UNITED STATES NAVY PATCHES

SHIPS / AD / AE / AF / BB / CG / DD / FF / LSD / LST / ETC.

MICHAEL L. ROBERTS

Schiffer Military/Aviation History
Atglen, PA

Acknowledgements

I would like to recognize a few friends that are authorities on naval ships:

Hank Ackerman	Hans Gross	Karl Mueller
Ken Britton	Michael Heidkamp	Herwig Plateau
Ludger Brockmann	Frank Jackson Jr.	Harold Rubin
Jackie De Bruyne	Peter Kraft	Doug Siegfried
Jim Filkosky	P. MacAuley	Michael Smolinski
Bruno De Groote	William Mezoff Jr.	

The patches depicted in this book are from the author's personal collection and are presented to serve as a guide for historians, and collectors.

This book is not intended to be the complete authority on the subject. It depicts over 1660 patches from World War II to the present. Aircraft carriers are covered in volume one of this series, and submarines are covered in volume six.

The images on pages 6, the front cover and endsheets are official U.S. Navy photographs.

Book Design by Michael L. Roberts & Robert Biondi.

Copyright © 1997 by Michael L. Roberts.
Library of Congress Catalog Number: 96-69998

Printed in Hong Kong.
ISBN: 0-7643-0144-6

We are interested in hearing from authors with book ideas on related topics.

Published by Schiffer Publishing Ltd.
77 Lower Valley Road
Atglen, PA 19310
Phone: (610) 593-1777
FAX: (610) 593-2002
Please write for a free catalog.
This book may be purchased from the publisher.
Please include $2.95 postage.
Try your bookstore first.

FOREWORD

Insignias are the modern form of heraldry of the knights of old. In the armed services insignias serve as a form of shorthand that iden-tifies an individual's service, rank, authority, specialty and organization. The organizational insignia, from the plain to very involved design, expresses a pride in oneself and his or her organization. From this pride springs self-discipline, the essence of respect for self, for service and for country.

The first semi-official Navy organizational insignias began to appear in the fledging Naval Aeronautical Organization in the early twenties with the establishment of the Bureau of Aeronautics in 1921 and a year later the formation of fighting, scouting, observation, seaplane patrol and torpedo plane squadrons. By 1927, the now familiar High Hat, Felix the Cat and VF-2's Flying Chiefs squadron insignias began appearing on the sides of the Navy's nimble, brightly colored biplane fighters. By the beginning of World War II all Navy aviation squadrons, most Naval and Reserve air stations, and even aircraft carriers had distinctive insignias.

During the Second World War aviation squadrons, surface ships and submarines, and shore establishment organizational insignias abound, establishing a high esprit de corps within each individual in that unit. Donald Duck, Mickey Mouse, Bugs Bunny and a host of other characters truly went to war with all branches of the armed services on the sides of tanks, planes and ships bridges. In fact in 1943, the Navy told its squadrons to knock off using Donald Duck so often for proposed insignias.

I remember all the displays of insignias in *Life* Magazine ads and collecting bottle caps and stickers from boxes of cereal during the war that had aviation insignias on them. We all knew what the insignias of the Flying Tigers, Eagle squadron, 94th Fighter and VF-31 squadrons looked like, what kind of planes they flew and how they performed in combat. When I grew up I was able turn my childhood dream into reality when I became a Naval Aviator. Acquiring that first patch in Training Squadron One and having it sewn on my flight jacket meant I had arrived and was truly a part of that unit. As my career progressed, so did the number of patches on my flight jacket until I ran out of room. Each patch on my jacket, as well as those that adorn the jackets of my fellow Naval Aviators, aircrew, and squadron/ship mates have a special memory and, in many cases, a long history behind them.

My interest in insignias is historical and I was fortunate to be able to continue to gather information on Navy and Marine Corps aviation organizations while I was in the Navy. Frequent trips to Washington, D.C., allowed me to spend considerable time at the Naval Air and Operational Histories offices where I collected as much information as I could on Navy/ Marine squadrons. I have been lucky to be able to be in a position to share much of this information as insignia editor for THE HOOK magazine, the Tailhook Association's quarterly journal of carrier aviation. In this capacity I have produced the magazine's patch page, a feature for 16 years, and answered all insignia inquiries. I quickly learned that it is next to impossible to identify every insignia because there are so many, and many are unidentifiable, even with the help of the historians at the Naval Air History office where all Navy aviation insignias are supposed to be officially approved.

This book serves as a valuable guide for the insignia collector and lovers of Navy patches in providing color pictures of past and present active and Reserve Navy aviation squadrons, ships, aircraft and shore organizations. It will help the serious collectors and those getting started to identify patches in their collections. Mike's collection of Navy insignias is vast and I thank him for sharing his collection with all of us.

Doug Siegfried, CDR USN (Ret)
THE HOOK Magazine
Insignia Editor

CONTENTS

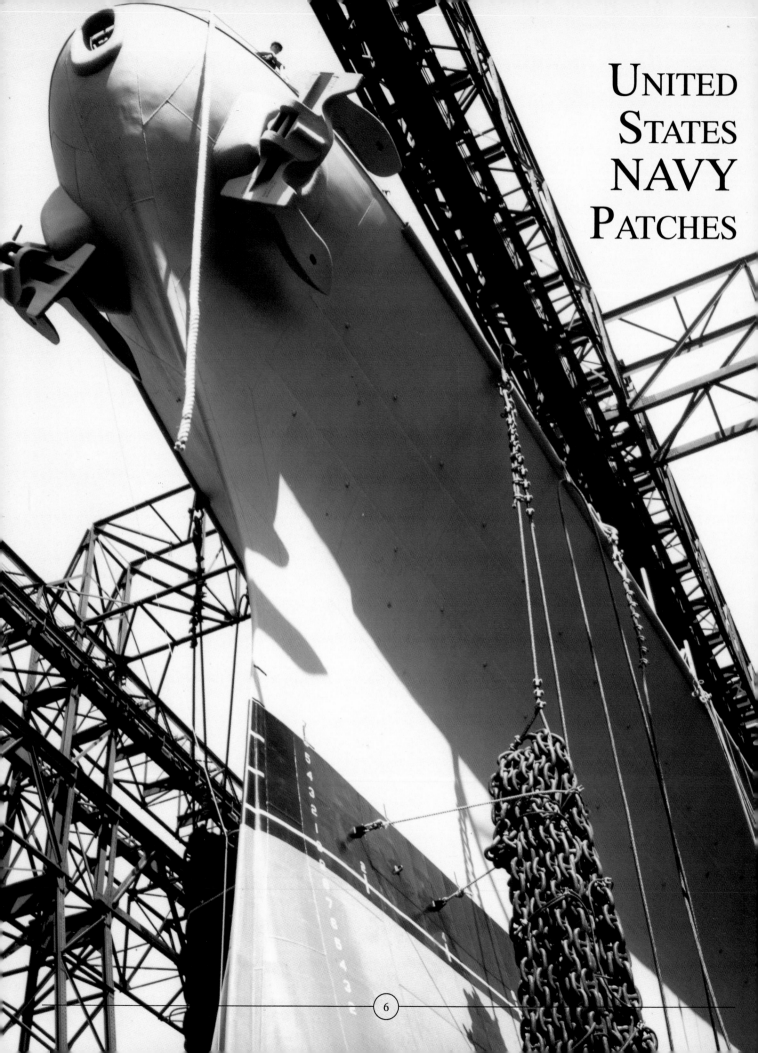

USS Dixie (AD-14)   USS Prairie (AD-15)

                                      USS Prairie (AD-15), 50th Anniversary

USS Cascade (AD-16)   USS Piedmont (AD-17)

USS Piedmont (AD-17)   USS Sierra (AD-18)   USS Sierra (AD-18)   USS Sierra (AD-18)

AD

USS Sierra (AD-18), Mediterranean Cruise, 1987-1988   USS Yosemite (AD-19)

USS Yosemite (AD-19)

USS Yosemite (AD-19)   USS Yosemite (AD-19), Mediterranean Cruise, 1974

AD

USS Yosemite (AD-19), Mediterranean Cruise, 1974

USS Yosemite (AD-19), Mediterranean/Indian Ocean, 1983-1984
USS Arcadia (AD-23)

USS Yosemite (AD-19), Mediterranean, 1988   USS Hamul (AD-20)   USS Everglades (AD-24)

AD

USS Shenandoah (AD-26) USS Yellowstone (AD-27) USS Isle Royal (AD-29)

USS Tidewater (AD-31) USS Bryce Canyon (AD-36) USS Bryce Canyon (AD-36), "E" Second Award

USS Samuel Gompers (AD-37) USS Samuel Gompers (AD-37) USS Samuel Gompers (AD-37)

AD

USS Samuel Gompers (AD-37)   USS Samuel Gompers (AD-37)   USS Samuel Gompers (AD-37)

USS Puget Sound (AD-38)   USS Yellowstone (AD-41)   USS Acadia (AD-42)

USS Acadia (AD-42)   USS Acadia (AD-42), Operation Desert Shield, 1990   USS Cape Cod (AD-43)

AD

USS Cape Cod (AD-43)　　　USS Cape Cod (AD-43), Westpac, 1994-1995　　　USS Shenandoah (AD-44)

USS Shasta (AE-6)　　　USS Firedrake (AE-14)　　　USS Vesuvius (AE-15)

USS Mount Katmai (AE-16)　　　USS Sitkin (AE-17)　　　USS Paricutin (AE-18)

AE

USS Diamond Head (AE-19)

USS Suribachi (AE-21)

USS Mauna Kea (AE-22)

USS Nitro (AE-23)

USS Nitro (AE-23)

USS Nitro (AE-23)

USS Nitro (AE-23), Operation Desert Storm, 1990-1991

USS Pyro (AE-24)

USS Haleakala (AE-25)

AE

USS Haleakala (AE-25)   USS Haleakala (AE-25)

USS Kilauea (AE-26)   USS Butte (AE-27)   USS Santa Barbara (AE-28)

USS Santa Barbara (AE-28)   USS Mount Hood (AE-29)   USS Mount Hood (AE-29)

USS Virgo (AE-30)

AE

USS Virgo (AE-30)	USS Chara (AE-31)	USS Flint (AE-32)
USS Shasta (AE-33)	USS Shasta (AE-33)	USS Mount Baker (AE-34)
USS Kiska (AE-35)	USS Kiska (AE-35)	USS Kiska (AE-35)

AE

USS Kiska (AE-35), Westpac 1988-1989   USS Alstede (AF-48)

USS Zelima (AF-49)   USS Arcturus (AF-52)   USS Pictor (AF-54)

USS Denebola (AF-56)   USS Regulus (AF-57)   USS Rigel (AF-58)

AF

USS Vega (AF-59)	USS Procyon (AF-61)	USS Los Alamos (AFDB-7)
USS Dynamic (AFDL-6)	USS Competent (AFDM-6)	USS Sustain (AFDM-7)
USS Sustain (AFDM-7)	USS Richland (AFDM-8)	USS Resolute (AFDM-10)

AFDM

USS Steadfast (AFDM-14)   USS Mars (AFS-1)   USS Mars (AFS-1), Operation Desert Storm, 1990-1991

USS Sylvania (AFS-2)   USS Niagara Falls (AFS-3)   USS Niagara Falls (AFS-3)

USS Niagara Falls (AFS-3), Operation Desert Storm, 1990-1991   USS White Plains (AFS-4)

AFS

USS Concord (AFS-5)   USS Concord (AFS-5) Mediterranean/Indian Ocean, 1983
USS Concord (AFS-5), Mediterranean, 1991-1992

USS San Diego (AFS-6)   USS San Diego (AFS-6), Operation Desert Shield, 1990   USS San Diego (AFS-6), Operation Desert Shield, 1990

AFS

USS San Jose (AFS-7)   USS San Jose (AFS-7)   USS San Jose (AFS-7), Change of Home Port, 1981

USS Compass Island (AG-153) USS Observation Island (AG-154) USS Oxford (AG-159)

USS Alacrity (AG-520)   USS Assurance (AG-521) USS Burton Island (AGB-1), Arctic Dew Line Operation, 1958

AGB

USS Atka (AGB-3) USS El Dorado (AGC-11) USS Glover (AGDE-1)

USS Point Loma (AGDS-2) USS Plainview (AGEH-1) USS Banner (AGER-1)

USS Pueblo (AGER-2) USS Pueblo (AGER-2), Recovery Team, 1968

AGER

USS Valcour (AGF-1), Arabian Gulf	USS La Salle (AGF-3)	USS La Salle (AGF-3), Persian Gulf Yacht Club
USS La Salle (AGF-3)	USS Coronado (AGF-11)	USS Coronado (AGF-11)
USS Glover (AGFF-1)	USS Arlington (AGMR-2)	USS Graham County (AGP-1176)

AGP

USS Investigator (AGR-9)

USS Interdictor (AGR-13)

USS Watchman (AGR-16)

USS Maury (AGS-16)

USS Requisite (AGS-18)

USS Rehoboth (AGS-50)

USS Oxford (AGTR-1)

USS Georgetown (AGTR-2)

USS Jamestown (AGTR-3)

AGTR

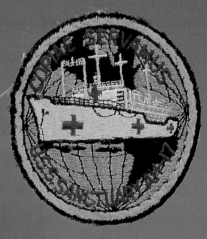

USS Liberty (AGTR-5)	USS Repose (AH-16)	USS Sanctuary (AH-17)
	USS Sanctuary (AH-17)	USS Oberon (AKA-14)
USS Thuban (AKA-19)	USS Muliphen (AKA-61)	USS Yancey (AKA-93)

AKA

USS Mathews (AKA-96)	USS Rankin (AKA-103)	USS Seminole (AKA-104)
USS Skagit (AKA-105)	USS Vermilion (AKA-107)	USS Washburn (AKA-108)
USS Tulare (AKA-112)	USS Mark (AKL-12)	USS Castor (AKS-1)

AKS

USS Proton (AKS-28)   USS Altair (AKS-32)

USS Butternut (AN-9)

USS Butternut (AN-9)   USS Cimarron (AO-22)   USS Platte (AO-24)

AO

USS Chemung (AO-30) USS Guadalupe (AO-32) USS Kennebec (AO-36)

USS Maccaponi (AO-41), Vietnam, 1965 USS Tappahannock (AO-43) USS Neches (AO-47)

USS Ashtabula (AO-51) USS Cacapon (AO-52)

AO

USS Chikaskia (AO-54)	USS Aucilla (AO-56)	USS Manatee (AO-58)
USS Severn (AO-61)	USS Allagash (AO-97)	USS Caloosahatchee (AO-98)
USS Canisteo (AO-99)	USS Mispillion (AO-105)	USS Passumpsic (AO-107)

AO

USS Pawcatuck (AO-108)

USS Waccamaw (AO-109)

USS Neosho (AO-143)

USS Neosho (AO-143)

USS Mississinewa (AO-144)

USS Hassayampa (AO-145)

USS Kawishiwi (AO-146)

USS Truckee (AO-147)

AO

USS Ponchatoula (AO-148)	USS Ponchatoula (AO-148), "E"	USS Cimarron (AO-177)
USS Monongahela (AO-178)	USS Merrimack (AO-179)	USS Willamette (AO-180)
USS Platte (AO-186)	USS Sacramento (AOE-1)	USS Sacramento (AOE-1)

AOE

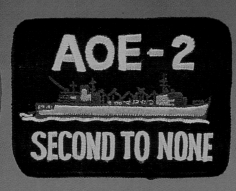

USS Sacramento (AOE-1), Operation Desert Storm, 1990-1991   USS Camden (AOE-2)   USS Camden (AOE-2)

USS Camden (AOE-2), Westpac, 1979   USS Camden (AOE-2)   USS Seattle (AOE-3)

USS Seattle (AOE-3)   USS Seattle (AOE-3), Mediterranean/Indian Ocean, 1981   USS Detroit (AOE-4)

AOE

USS Detroit (AOE-4), Red Sea, 1990   USS Detroit (AOE-4), Mediterranean   USS Detroit (AOE-4), Mediterranean

USS Supply (AOE-6)   USS Sakatonchee (AOG-19)   USS Chewaucan (AOG-50)

USS Noxubee (AOG-56)   USS Wichita (AOR-1)   USS Wichita (AOR-1)

AOR

USS Wichita (AOR-1)   USS Wichita (AOR-1), Battle Group Echo, 1983-1984   USS Milwaukee (AOR-2)

USS Milwaukee (AOR-2)   USS Kansas City (AOR-3)   USS Kansas City (AOR-3)

USS Kansas City (AOR-3), Operation Desert Storm, 1990-1991   USS Savannah (AOR-4)   USS Wabash (AOR-5)

AOR

USS Wabash (AOR-5)	USS Kalamazoo (AOR-6)	USS Roanoke (AOR-7)
USS Roanoke (AOR-7)	USS Hunter Liggett (APA-14)	USS American Legion (APA-17)
USS George Clymer (APA-27)	USS Monrovia (APA-31)	USS Bayfield (APA-33)

APA

USS Cavalier (APA-37)	USS Elmore (APA-42)	USS Henrico (APA-45)
USS Hansford (APA-106)	USS Lena (APA-195)	USS Magoffin (APA-199)
USS Telfair (APA-210)	USS Mountrail (APA-213)	USS Navarro (APA-215)

APA

USS Noble (APA-218)

USS Pickaway (APA-222)

USS Renville (APA-227)

USS Rockbridge (APA-228)

USS Paul Revere (APA-248)

USS Benewah (APB-35)

USS Ruchamkin (APD-89)

USS Cook (APD-130)

USS Weiss (APD-135)

APD

USS Vulcan (AR-5)	USS Vulcan (AR-5)	USS Ajax (AR-6)
USS Hector (AR-7)	USS Hector (AR-7)	USS Jason (AR-8)
USS Jason (AR-8)	USS Jason (AR-8)	USS Delta (AR-9)

AR

USS Amphion (AR-13)   USS Cadmus (AR-14)   USS Klondike (AR-22)

USS Markab (AR-23)   USS Grand Canyon (AR-28)   USS De Mayo (ARA-25)

USS Neptune (ARC-2)   USS Aeolus (ARC-3)   USS Waterford (ARD-5)

ARD

USS Waterford (ARD-5), 50th Anniversary, 1942-1992   USS West Milton (ARD-7)   USS White Sands (ARD-20)

USS San Onofre (ARD-30)   USS —— (ARD BS-20)   USS Oak Ridge (ARDM-1)

USS Oak Ridge (ARDM-1)   USS Alamogordo (ARDM-2)   USS Shippingport (ARDM-4)

ARDM

USS Arco (ARDM-5)	USS Tutuila (ARG-4), Vietnam	USS Satyr (ARL-23)
USS Sphinx (ARL-24)	USS Askari (ARL-30)	USS Escape (ARS-6)
USS Escape (ARS-6)	USS Preserver (ARS-8)	USS Deliver (ARS-23)

ARS

USS Safeguard (ARS-25)	USS Bolster (ARS-38)	USS Hoist (ARS-40)
USS Hoist (ARS-40)	USS Opportune (ARS-41)	USS Opportune (ARS-41)
USS Reclaimer (ARS-42)	USS Reclaimer (ARS-42)	USS Safeguard (ARS-50)

ARS

USS Grasp (ARS-51)

USS Salvor (ARS-52)

USS Grapple (ARS-53)

USS Grapple (ARS-53), Mediterranean, 1992

USS Fulton (AS-11)

USS Sperry (AS-12)

USS Pelias (AS-14)

USS Bushnell (AS-15)

USS Howard W. Gilmore (AS-16)

AS

USS Howard W. Gilmore (AS-16)	USS Nereus (AS-17)	USS Orion (AS-18)
USS Orion (AS-18)	USS Proteus (AS-19)	USS Proteus (AS-19)
USS Proteus (AS-19)	USS Hunley (AS-31)	USS Hunley (AS-31)

AS

USS Hunley (AS-31), 25 Years	USS Holland (AS-32)	USS Holland (AS-32)
USS Holland (AS-32)	USS Holland (AS-32)	USS Holland (AS-32)
USS Simon Lake (AS-33)	USS Simon Lake (AS-33)	USS Canopus (AS-34)

AS

USS L.Y. Spear (AS-36)   USS L.Y. Spear (AS-36), Persian Gulf, 1991   USS Dixon (AS-37)

USS Emory S. Land (AS-39)   USS Emory S. Land (AS-39)   USS Frank Cable (AS-40)

USS Frank Cable (AS-40)   USS McKee (AS-41)

AS

USS McKee (AS-41), Northpac, 1987   USS McKee (AS-41)   USS McKee (AS-41)

USS Coucal (ASR-8)   USS Florikan (ASR-9)   USS Florikan (ASR-9)

USS Florican (ASR-9)   USS Greenlet (ASR-10)

ASR

USS Kittiwake (ASR-13)   USS Kittiwake (ASR-13)   USS Petrel (ASR-14)

USS Petrel (ASR-14)

USS Petrel (ASR-14)   USS Sunbird (ASR-15)

USS Sunbird (ASR-15)

ASR

USS Tringa (ASR-16)	USS Tringa (ASR-16)	USS Skylark (ASR-20)
USS Pigeon (ASR-21)	USS Pigeon (ASR-21)	USS Pigeon (ASR-21)
USS Ortolan (ASR-22)	USS Ortolan (ASR-22)	USS Ortolan (ASR-22)

ASR

USS Ortolan (ASR-22)   USS Tillamook (ATA-192)   USS Tatnuck (ATA-195)

USS Sunnadin (ATA-197)   USS Wandank (ATA-204)   USS Catawba (ATA-210)

USS Apache (ATF-67)   USS Kiowa (ATF-72)   USS Sioux (ATF-75)

ATF

USS Chickasaw (ATF-83)   USS Cree (ATF-84)   USS Mataco (ATF-86)

USS Tawasa (ATF-92)   USS Abnaki (ATF-96)   USS Chowanoc (ATF-100)

USS Hitchiti (ATF-103)   USS Moctobi (ATF-105)

ATF

USS Moctobi (ATF-105)   USS Moctobi (ATF-105)   USS Molala (ATF-106)

USS Molala (ATF-106)   USS Quapaw (ATF-110)

USS Quapaw (ATF-110)   USS Takelma (ATF-113)   USS Tawakoni (ATF-114)

ATF

USS Tawakoni (ATF-114)   USS Luiseno (ATF-156)   USS Nipmuc (ATF-157)

USS Paiute (ATF-159)   USS Papago (ATF-160)   USS Salinan (ATF-161)

USS Utina (ATF-163)   USS —— (ATR-50)

ATR

USS Edenton (ATS-1)   USS Beaufort (ATS-2)   USS Beaufort (ATS-2)

USS Brunswick (ATS-3)   USS Brunswick (ATS-3)   USS Currituck (AV-7)

USS Pine Island (AV-12), Far East Cruise, 1960-1961   USS Tallahatchie County (AVB-2)

AVB

USS Norton Sound (AVM-1)

USS Norton Sound (AVM-1)

USS Duxbury Bay (AVP-38)

USS Orca (AVP-49)

USS Arizona (BB-39)

USS North Carolina (BB-55)

USS South Dakota (BB-57)

USS Alabama (BB-60)

BB

USS Iowa (BB-61)	USS Iowa (BB-61)	USS Iowa (BB-61), Mediterranean/Indian Ocean, 1987-1988
USS New Jersey (BB-62)	USS New Jersey (BB-62)	USS New Jersey (BB-62)
USS New Jersey (BB-62)	USS New Jersey (BB-62)	USS New Jersey (BB-62), Beirut, Lebanon

BB

USS New Jersey (BB-62), Westpac, 1983

USS New Jersey (BB-62), Westpac/Northpac, 1986

USS New Jersey (BB-62), Beirut, Lebanon, 1983-1984

USS New Jersey (BB-62), Westpac, 1989-1990

USS New Jersey (BB-62), Veterans

USS Missouri (BB-63)

USS Missouri (BB-63)

USS Missouri (BB-63)

USS Missouri (BB-63)

BB

USS Missouri (BB-63)   USS Missouri (BB-63), Rimpac, 1990   USS Missouri (BB-63), Operation Desert Shield, 1990

USS Missouri (BB-63), Operation Desert Storm, 1990-1991   USS Missouri (BB-63), Operation Desert Storm, 1990-1991
USS Missouri (BB-63), Operation Desert Storm, 1990-1991

USS Wisconsin (BB-64)   USS Wisconsin (BB-64)   USS Wisconsin (BB-64), Westpac, 1951-1954

BB

USS Wisconsin (BB-64), 50th Anniversary, 1944-1994   USS Boston (CA-69)   USS St. Paul (CA-73)

USS Helena (CA-75)   USS Toledo (CA-133)   USS Los Angeles (CA-135)

USS Newport News (CA-148)   USS Newport News (CA-148)   USS Boston (CAG-1)

CAG

USS Alaska (CB-1)	USS Northampton (CC-1)	USS Wright (CC-2)
USS Little Rock (CG-4)	USS Oklahoma City (CG-5)	USS Albany (CG-10)
USS Albany (CG-10)	USS Chicago (CG-11)	USS Columbus (CG-12)

CG

USS Leahy (CG-16)   USS Leahy (CG-16), Ancient Order of the Deep   USS Leahy (CG-16)

USS Harry E. Yarnell (CG-17)   USS Harry E. Yarnell (CG-17), Indian Ocean,1983-1984   USS Worden (CG-18)

USS Worden (CG-18), Operation Desert Shield, 1990-1991   USS Dale (CG-19)

CG

USS Dale (CG-19), Mediterranean, 1991   USS Dale (CG-19), Mediterranean, 1991   USS Richard K. Turner (CG-20)

USS Richard K. Turner (CG-20), Persian Gulf, 1987-1988   USS Richard K. Turner (CG-20)   USS Gridley (CG-21)

USS Gridley (CG-21)   USS Gridley (CG-21)   USS Gridley (CG-21)

CG

USS Gridley (CG-21), 1981-1982	USS England (CG-22)	USS England (CG-22)
USS England (CG-22), Rimpac/Westpac, 1982	USS Halsey (CG-23)	USS Halsey (CG-23)
USS Halsey (CG-23), Ancient Order of the Deep	USS Reeves (CG-24)	USS Belknap (CG-26)

CG

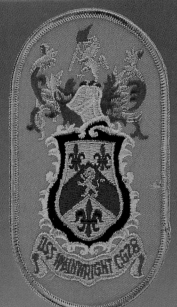

USS Belknap (CG-26)	USS Belknap (CG-26)	USS Josephus Daniels (CG-27)
USS Josephus Daniels (CG-27)	USS Wainwright (CG-28)	USS Wainwright (CG-28)
USS Jouett (CG-29)	USS Jouett (CG-29)	USS Horne (CG-30)

CG

USS Horne (CG-30), Westpac, 1987-1988   USS Horne (CG-30), Det.21   USS Sterett (CG-31)

USS Sterett (CG-31)   USS William H. Standley (CG-32)   USS William H. Standley (CG-32)

USS William H. Standley (CG-32), 25 Years, 1966-1991   USS William H. Standley (CG-32)

USS William H. Standley (CG-32), Ancient Order of the Deep

CG

USS Fox (CG-33) USS Fox (CG-33) USS Fox (CG-33), Persian Gulf, 1987

USS Fox (CG-33), Persian Gulf, 1988 USS Fox (CG-33), Persian Gulf, 1989 USS Fox (CG-33)

USS Fox (CG-33), Outboard II USS Biddle (CG-34)

CG

USS Biddle (CG-34) USS Biddle (CG-34) USS Truxton (CG-35)

USS Ticonderoga (CG-47) USS Ticonderoga (CG-47), First Aegis Cruiser Overhaul, 1992-1993 USS Yorktown (CG-48)

USS Yorktown (CG-48), Shock Trials USS Yorktown (CG-48), Mediterranean Cruise, 1991 USS Vincennes (CG-49)

CG

USS Vincennes (CG-49)   USS Vincennes (CG-49)   USS Vincennes (CG-49), Persian Gulf Yacht Club

USS Vincennes (CG-49)   USS Vincennes (CG-49), Gulf Games, 1988   USS Vincennes (CG-49), Westpac, 1990

USS Valley Forge (CG-50)   USS Valley Forge (CG-50)   USS Valley Forge (CG-50), Pacex, Northern Pacific, 1989

CG

USS Valley Forge (CG-50), Operation Desert Shield, 1990-1991   USS Thomas S. Gates (CG-51), Sevastopol, Russia, 1989

USS Thomas S. Gates (CG-51)

USS Bunker Hill (CG-52)   USS Bunker Hill (CG-52)   USS Bunker Hill (CG-52), 50th Anniversary, 1942-1992

USS Bunker Hill (CG-52), Arabian Gulf Battle Force   USS Bunker Hill (CG-52), Operation Desert Storm, 1990-1991

USS Bunker Hill (CG-52), Operation Desert Shield, 1990

CG

USS Mobile Bay (CG-53)

USS Mobile Bay (CG-53)

USS Mobile Bay (CG-53), Westpac, 1992

USS Mobile Bay (CG-53), Westpac, 1992

USS Mobile Bay (CG-53), Persian Gulf Cruise, 1993-1994

USS Antietam (CG-54)

USS Antietam (CG-54)

USS Leyte Gulf (CG-55)

USS Leyte Gulf (CG-55), Mediterranean Cruise, 1989

CG

USS Leyte Gulf (CG-55), Operation Desert Storm, 1990-1991   USS San Jacinto (CG-56)

USS Leyte Gulf (CG-55), Red Sea, 1991

USS San Jacinto (CG-56), Operation Desert Storm, 1990-1991   USS Lake Champlain (CG-57)

USS San Jacinto (CG-56), UNITAS XXXIII, 1992

USS Philippines Sea (CG-58)   USS Philippines Sea (CG-58), Mediterranean Cruise, 1990-1991

USS Philippines Sea (CG-58)

CG

USS Philippines Sea (CG-58), Operation Desert Shield, 1990-1991

USS Princeton (CG-59), Westpac 1990

USS Princeton (CG-59)

USS Princeton (CG-59), Rimpac, 1990

USS Princeton (CG-59), Operation Desert Shield, 1990

USS Normandy (CG-60)

USS Monterey (CG-61)

USS Normandy (CG-60), Operation Desert Storm, 1991

CG

USS Monterey (CG-61)

USS Monterey (CG-61), Mediterranean/Black Sea, 1991-1992

USS Monterey (CG-61), Mediterranean Cruise, 1991-1992

USS Chancellorsville (CG-62)

USS Cowpens (CG-63)

USS Cowpens (CG-63), Shellback, 1993

USS Gettysburg (CG-64)

USS Chosin (CG-65)

CG

USS Chosin (CG-65), Westpac, 1992   USS Hue City (CG-66)   USS Shiloh (CG-67)

USS Shiloh (CG-67)   USS Anzio (CG-68)   USS Vicksburg (CG-69)

USS Lake Erie (CG-70)   USS Lake Erie (CG-70), Pearl Harbor Cruise, 1993   USS Cape St. George (CG-71)

CG

USS Vella Gulf (CG-72)

USS Port Royal (CG-73)

USS Long Beach (CGN-9)

USS Long Beach (CGN-9), Westpac, 1991

USS Truxton (CGN-35)

USS Truxton (CGN-35), Northpac, 1987

USS California (CGN-36)

USS South carolina (CGN-37)

USS Virginia (CGN-38)

CGN

USS Texas (CGN-39)   USS Mississippi (CGN-40)   USS Arkansas (CGN-41)

USS Arkansas (CGN-41), Persian Gulf, 1991   USS Raleigh (CL-7)

USS Savannah (CL-42)   USS Honolulu (CL-48)

CL

USS San Diego (CL-53)   USS Columbia (CL-56)   USS Biloxi (CL-80)

USS Manchester (CL-83), Korea   USS Roanoke (CL-145)   USS Galvaston (CLG-3)

USS Little Rock (CLG-4)   USS Providence (CLG-6)

CLG

USS Springfield (CLG-7)   USS Topeka (CLG-8)   USS Phelps (DD-360)

USS Rowan (DD-405)   USS Radford (DD-446)   USS O'Bannon (DD-450)

USS Chevalier (DD-451)   USS Ellison (DD-454)

DD

USS Laffey (DD-459), Presidential Unit Citation

USS Waller (DD-466)

USS Bache (DD-470)

USS Renshaw (DD-499)

USS Kimberly (DD-521)

USS Mullany (DD-528)

USS Hazelwood (DD-531)

USS John Paul Jones (DD-532)

USS The Sullivans (DD-537)

DD

USS Twining (DD-540)   USS Cowell (DD-547)   USS Prichett (DD-561)

USS Ross (DD-563)   USS Stoddard (DD-566)   USS Wren (DD-568)

USS Gansevoort (DD-608)   USS Abbott (DD-629)   USS Erben (DD-631)

DD

USS Hale (DD-642)   USS Cogswell (DD-651)   USS Ingersoll (DD-652)

USS Ingersoll (DD-652)   USS Bearss (DD-654)   USS Dashiell (DD-659)

USS Black (DD-666)   USS Black (DD-666)   USS Chauncey (DD-667)

DD

USS Dortch (DD-670)   USS Hickox (DD-673)   USS Hunt (DD-674)

USS Marshall (DD-676)   USS Picking (DD-685)   USS Halsey Powell (DD-686)

USS Uhlmann (DD-687)   USS Remey (DD-688)

DD

USS Allen M. Sumner (DD-692)	USS M Dale (DD-693)	USS Ingraham (DD-694)
USS English (DD-696)	USS Charles S. Sperry (DD-697)	USS Charles S. Sperry (DD-697), Westpac, 1965-1966
USS Ault (DD-698)	USS Waldron (DD-699)	USS W.L. Lind (DD-703)

DD

USS Borie (DD-704) USS Compton (DD-705) USS Gainard (DD-706)

USS Harlan R. Dickson (DD-708) USS Hugh Purvis (DD-709), cap patch USS Gearing (DD-710)

USS Eugene A. Greene (DD-711) USS Kenneth D. Bailey (DD-713)

DD

USS William R. Rush (DD-714)

USS William M. Wood (DD-715)

USS Wiltsie (DD-716)

USS Theodore E. Chandler (DD-717)

USS Hamner (DD-718)

USS Epperson (DD-719)

USS Barton (DD-722)

USS Walke (DD-723)

USS Laffey (DD-724)

DD

USS O'Brien (DD-725)   USS De Haven (DD-727)   USS Mansfield (DD-728)

USS Lyman K. Swenson (DD-729)   USS Collett (DD-730)   USS Maddox (DD-731)

USS Purdy (DD-734)   USS Blue (DD-744)   USS Southerland (DD-745)

DD

USS Samuel N. Moore (DD-747) USS Harry E. Hubbard (DD-748) USS John R. Pierce (DD-753)

USS Frank E. Evans (DD-754) USS Strong (DD-758) USS Lofberg (DD-759)

USS John W. Thomason (DD-760) USS Buck (DD-761)

DD

USS Buck (DD-761)	USS Henley (DD-762)	USS William C. Lawe (DD-763)
USS Lloyd Thomas (DD-764)	USS Keppler (DD-765)	USS James C. Owens (DD-776)
USS Zellars (DD-777)	USS R.K. Huntington (DD-781)	USS Rowan (DD-782)

DD

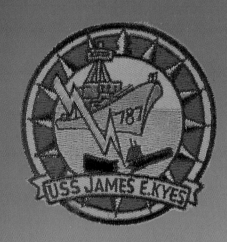

USS Gurke (DD-783)

USS McKean (DD-784)

USS Henderson (DD-785)

USS Richard B. Anderson (DD-786)

USS James E. Kyes (DD-787)

USS James E. Kyes (DD-787)

USS Hollister (DD-788)

USS Eversole (DD-789)

USS Shelton (DD-790)

DD

USS Cassin Young (DD-793)   USS Benham (DD-796)   USS Colhoun (DD-801)

USS Gregory (DD-802)   USS Rooks (DD-804)

USS Chevalier (DD-805)

USS Higbee (DD-806)   USS Corry (DD-817)

DD

USS New (DD-818)   USS Holder (DD-819)   USS Holder (DD-819), NATO Standing Naval Force, 1968

USS Rich (DD-820)   USS Johnston (DD-821)   USS Johnston (DD-821)

USS R.H. McCard (DD-822)   USS Samuel B. Roberts (DD-823)   USS Basilone (DD-824)

DD

USS Carpenter (DD-825)

USS Agerholm (DD-826)

USS Robert A. Owens (DD-827)

USS Timmerman (DD-828)

USS Myles C. Fox (DD-829)

USS Herbert J. Thomas (DD-833)

USS Charles P. Cecil (DD-835)

USS George K. Mackenzie (DD-836)

USS George K. Mackenzie (DD-836), "E" and "A"

DD

USS Sarsfield (DD-837)	USS Power (DD-839)	USS Glennon (DD-840)
USS Noa (DD-841)	USS Noa (DD-841)	USS Fiske (DD-842)
USS Warrington (DD-843)	USS Bausell (DD-845)	USS Bausell (DD-845)

DD

USS Ozbourn (DD-846)   USS Robert Wilson (DD-847)   USS R.E. Kraus (DD-849)

USS Joseph P. Kennedy, Jr. (DD-850)   USS Joseph P. Kennedy, Jr. (DD-850)   USS Rupertus (DD-851)

USS Charles H. Roan (DD-853)   USS Bristol (DD-857)   USS Fred T. Berry (DD-858)

DD

USS Norris (DD-859)	USS McCaffery (DD-860)	USS Vogelgesang (DD-862)
USS Steinaker (DD-863)	USS Harold J. Ellison (DD-864)	USS Charles R. Ware (DD-865)
USS Cone (DD-866)	USS Cone (DD-866)	USS Stribling (DD-867)

DD

USS Brownson (DD-868)	USS Arnold J. Isbell (DD-869)	USS Damato (DD-871)
USS Forrest Royal (DD-872)	USS Hawkins (DD-873)	USS Duncan (DD-874)
USS Henry W. Tucker (DD-875)	USS Rogers (DD-876)	USS Perkins (DD-877)

DD

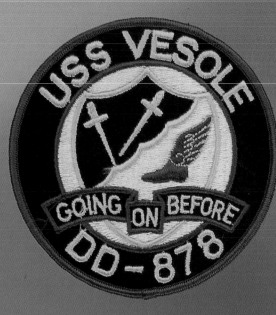

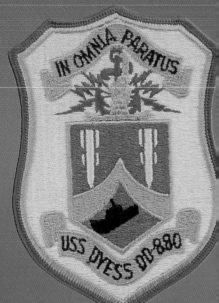

USS Vesole (DD-878)	USS Leary (DD-879)	USS Dyess (DD-880)
USS Dyess (DD-880)	USS Dyess (DD-880)	USS Bordelon (DD-881)
USS Furse (DD-882)	USS N.K. Perry (DD-883)	

DD

USS Floyd B. Parks (DD-881)

USS Orleck (DD-886)

USS Brinkley Bass (DD-887)

USS Stickell (DD-888), Westpac, 1966

USS O'Hare (DD-889)

USS Meredith (DD-890)

USS Forrest Sherman (DD-931)

USS Forrest Sherman (DD-931)

USS Barry (DD-933)

DD

USS Davis (DD-937)	USS Jonas Ingram (DD-938)	USS Jonas Ingram (DD-938)
USS Manley (DD-940)	USS DuPont (DD-941)	USS DuPont (DD-941)
USS Bigelow (DD-942)	USS Blandy (DD-943)	USS Blandy (DD-943), Suez, 1982

DD

USS Mullinnix (DD-944)	USS Hull (DD-945)	USS Hull (DD-945)
USS Edson (DD-946)	USS Edson (DD-946)	USS Edson (DD-946)
USS Morton (DD-948)	USS Parsons (DD-949)	USS Richard S. Edwards (DD-950)

DD

USS Turner Joy (DD-951)   USS Turner Joy (DD-951)   USS Spruance (DD-963)

USS Paul F. Foster (DD-964)   USS Kinkaid (DD-965)   USS Kinkaid (DD-965), Ancient Order of the Deep

USS Hewitt (DD-966)   USS Hewitt (DD-966), 1983   USS Hewitt (DD-966)

DD

USS Elliot (DD-967) USS Elliot (DD-967) USS Arthur W. Radford (DD-968)

USS Arthur W. Radford (DD-968), Mediterranean Cruise, 1991-1992 USS Peterson (DD-969) USS Peterson (DD-969)

USS Peterson (DD-969), Middle East, 1993 USS Caron (DD-970)

DD

USS Caron (DD-970), Mediterranean, 1985   USS Caron (DD-970), Blue Harrier Europe, 1995   USS David R. Ray (DD-971)

USS David R. Ray (DD-971)   USS David R. Ray (DD-971), Operation Desert Shield, 1990   USS Oldendorf (DD-972)

USS Oldendorf (DD-972)   USS John Young (DD-973)

DD

USS John Young (DD-973)   USS John Young (DD-973), Arabian Gulf, 1992   USS Comte De Grasse (DD-974)

USS Comte De Grasse (DD-974)   USS Comte De Grasse (DD-974), "E", 1988

USS Comte De Grasse (DD-974), Standard Naval Force Atlantic, 1983

USS Comte De Grasse (DD-974), UNITUS XXXVI, 1995   USS O'Brien (DD-975)   USS O'Brien (DD-975), Persian Gulf, 1988

DD

USS O'Brien (DD-975), Westpac, 1990   USS Merrill (DD-976)   USS Merrill (DD-976)

USS Briscoe (DD-977)   USS Stump (DD-978)   USS Stump (DD-978)

USS Conolly (DD-979)   USS Moosbrugger (DD-980)   USS Moosbrugger (DD-980), Operation Desert Shield, 1990

DD

USS Moosbrugger (DD-980),
Operation Desert Shield, 1990
USS John Hancock (DD-981),
Mediterranean Cruise, 1991-1992
USS John Rodgers (DD-983)

USS John Hancock (DD-981)

USS Nicholson (DD-982)

USS John Rodgers (DD-983)

USS John Hancock (DD-981)

USS John Rodgers (DD-983)

USS John Rodgers (DD-983), Mediterranean Cruise, 1990

DD

USS Leftwich (DD-984)   USS Leftwich (DD-984)   USS Cushing (DD-985)

USS Cushing (DD-985), Around the Horn,   USS Harry W. Hill (DD-986)   USS Harry W. Hill (DD-986)
UNITAS XXXIII, 1992

USS Harry W. Hill (DD-986), Westpac, 1995-1996

DD

USS O'Bannon (DD-987)   USS O'Bannon (DD-987), Persian Gulf, 1995   USS Thorn (DD-988)

USS Thorn (DD-988)   USS Deyo (DD-989)   USS Deyo (DD-989), Mediterranean Cruise, 1991

USS Ingersoll (DD-990)   USS Fife (DD-991)   USS Fife (DD-991)

DD

USS Fletcher (DD-992) USS Fletcher (DD-992), Memorial Cruise/Reunion, 1988 USS Hayler (DD-997)

USS Nicholas (DDE-449) USS Conway (DDE-507)

USS Cony (DDE-508) USS Robert A. Owens (DDE-827) USS Fred T. Berry (DDE-858)

DDE

USS Charles F. Adams (DDG-2)   USS John King (DDG-3)   USS Lawrence (DDG-4)

USS Lawrence (DDG-4), UNITAS XXVII, 1986   USS Claude V. Ricketts (DDG-5), Mediterranean Cruise, 1976-1977

USS Claude V. Ricketts (DDG-5)

USS Claude V. Ricketts (DDG-5), Mediterranean, 1983-1984   USS Barney (DDG-6)   USS Barney (DDG-6)

DDG

USS Henry B. Wilson (DDG-7)   USS Henry B. Wilson (DDG-7)   USS Henry B. Wilson (DDG-7)   USS Henry B. Wilson (DDG-7)

USS Lynde McCormick (DDG-8)   USS Lynde McCormick (DDG-8)   USS Towers (DDG-9)

USS Sampson (DDG-10)   USS Sampson (DDG-10), Mediterranean Cruise, 1990-1991

DDG

USS Sampson (DDG-10), "E"   USS Sellers (DDG-11)   USS Sellers (DDG-11)

USS Robison (DDG-12)   USS Robison (DDG-12)   USS Hoel (DDG-13)

USS Buchanan (DDG-14)   USS Buchanan (DDG-14)

DDG

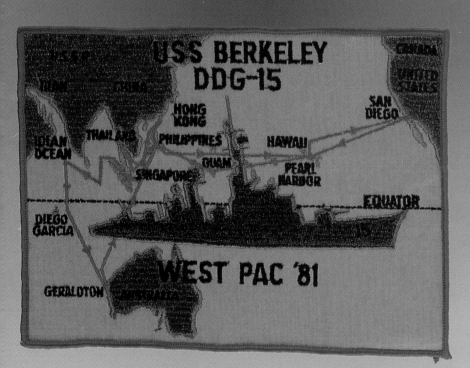

USS Berkeley (DDG-15)   USS Berkeley (DDG-15), Westpac, 1976

                              USS Berkeley (DDG-15), 1962-1992

USS Berkeley (DDG-15), Westpac, 1981   USS Joseph Strauss (DDG-16)

DDG

USS Joseph Strauss (DDG-16)   USS Conyngham (DDG-17)   USS Semmes (DDG-18)

USS Semmes (DDG-18)   USS Semmes (DDG-18), Mediterranean Cruise, 1968   USS Tattnall (DDG-19)

USS Goldsborough (DDG-20)   USS Goldsborough (DDG-20), Westpac, 1990

DDG

USS Goldsborough (DDG-20), Just Cruising, 1990   USS Cochrane (DDG-21)   USS Benjamin Stoddert (DDG-22)

USS Benjamin Stoddert (DDG-22), Westpac, 1982   USS Benjamin Stoddert (DDG-22), Westpac, 1983

USS Benjamin Stoddert (DDG-22), Westpac, 1988   USS Richard E. Byrd (DDG-23)   USS Richard E. Byrd (DDG-23)

DDG

USS Waddell (DDG-24)   USS Waddell (DDG-24)   USS Waddell (DDG-24)

USS Waddell (DDG-24)   USS Waddell (DDG-24)   USS Decatur (DDG-31)

USS Decatur (DDG-31), Australia/New Zealand, 1976   USS John Paul Jones (DDG-32)

DDG

USS Parsons (DDG-33)	USS Parsons (DDG-33)	USS Somers (DDG-34)
USS Mitscher (DDG-35)	USS John S. McCain (DDG-36)	USS Farragut (DDG-37)
USS Luce (DDG-38)		USS Luce (DDG-38)

DDG

USS MacDonough (DDG-39)   USS MacDonough (DDG-39)   USS Coontz (DDG-40)

USS King (DDG-41)   USS Mahan (DDG-42)   USS Mahan (DDG-42)

USS Dahlgren (DDG-43)   USS Dahlgren (DDG-43), Mediterranean, 1983

DDG

USS Dahlgren (DDG-43), UNITAS XXXII, 1991   USS William V. Pratt (DDG-44)   USS Dewey (DDG-45)

USS Preble (DDG-46)   USS Preble (DDG-46)   USS Arleigh Burke (DDG-51)

USS Arleigh Burke (DDG-51), Trial Bravo, 1991   USS Barry (DDG-52)   USS John Paul Jones (DDG-53)   USS John Paul Jones (DDG-53)

DDG

USS Curtis Wilbur (DDG-54) USS Curtis Wilbur (DDG-54), Westpac, 1995 USS Stout (DDG-55)

USS John S. McCain (DDG-56) USS Mitscher (DDG-57) USS Laboon (DDG-58)

USS Russell (DDG-59) USS Paul Hamilton (DDG-60) USS Ramage (DDG-61)

DDG

USS Fitzgerald (DDG-62), Construction Team

USS Fitzgerald (DDG-62)

USS Fitzgerald (DDG-62), Alpha Trials, 1995

USS Fitzgerald (DDG-62), Bravo Trials, 1995

USS Stethem (DDG-63)

USS Carney (DDG-64)

USS Benfold (DDG-65)

USS Gonzalez (DDG-66)

USS Cole (DDG-67)

DDG

USS Milius (DDG-69)   USS Hopper (DDG-70)   USS Kidd (DDG-993)

USS Kidd (DDG-993), Top Gun USS Kidd (DDG-993), Fifth Consecutive Battle "E" USS Kidd (DDG-993), Eastpac Cruise, 1992-1993

USS Kidd (DDG-993), USS Kidd (DDG-993), Mediterranean Cruise, 1994-1995 USS Callaghan (DDG-994)
Mediterranean Cruise, 1994-1995

DDG

USS Callaghan (DDG-994)   USS Callaghan (DDG-994), SWAT 17   USS Callaghan (DDG-994), Persian Gulf, 1988

USS Callaghan (DDG-994), World Cruise, 1992   USS Callaghan (DDG-994), Westpac, 1993-1994

USS Callaghan (DDG-994), Westpac, 1993-1994

USS Scott (DDG-995)   USS Scott (DDG-995)   USS Scott (DDG-995), North Atlantic Cruise, 1991

DDG

USS Chandler (DDG-996)

USS Chandler (DDG-996)

USS Eugene A. Greene (DDR-711)

USS W.R. Rush (DDR-714)

USS K.D. Bailey (DDR-713)

USS William M. Wood (DDR-715)

USS Higbee (DDR-806)

DDR

USS Dennis J. Buckley (DDR-808)   USS Myles C. Fox (DDR-829)   USS Everett F. Larson (DDR-830)

USS Goodrich (DDR-831)   USS Hanson (DDR-832), Coral Sea Celebration, 1963   USS Charles P. Cecil (DDR-835)

USS Ernest G. Small (DDR-838)   USS Rogers (DDR-876)   USS Vesole (DDR-878)

DDR

USS Leary (DDR-879)

USS Huse (DE-145)

USS Brough (DE-148)

USS William C. Miller (DE-259)

USS Woodson (DE-359)

USS Romback (DE-364)

USS McGinty (DE-365)

USS Charles E. Brannon (DE-446)

USS Whitehurst (DE-634)

DE

USS Wiseman (DE-667) USS Greenwood (DE-679) USS Coates (DE-685)

USS Marsh (DE-699) USS Marsh (DE-699) USS Parle (DE-708)

USS Kyne (DE-744) USS Weeden (DE-797), World War II USS Hammerberg (DE-1015)

DE

USS Courtney (DE-1021)   USS Lester (DE-1022)   USS Evans (DE-1023)

USS Bridget (DE-1024)   USS Bauer (DE-1025)   USS Hooper (DE-1026)

USS Joseph K. Taussig (DE-1030)   USS John R. Perry (DE-1034)   USS McMorris (DE-1036)

DE

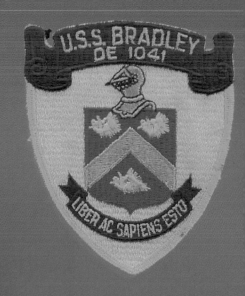

USS Bronstein (DE-1037)	USS McCloy (DE-1038)	USS Bradley (DE-1041)
USS Edward McDonnell (DE-1043)	USS Brumby (DE-1044)	USS Davidson (DE-1045)
USS Voge (DE-1047)	USS Sample (DE-1048)	USS Koelsch (DE-1049)

DE

USS Albert David (DE-1050)	USS O'Callahan (DE-1051)	USS Knox (DE-1052)
USS Roarke (DE-1053)	USS Gray (DE-1054)	USS Hepburn (DE-1055)
USS Connole (DE-1056)	USS Rathburne (DE-1057)	USS Meyerkord (DE-1058)

DE

USS W.S. Sims (DE-1059)　　　　USS Lang (DE-1060)　　　　USS Patterson (DE-1061)

USS Whipple (DE-1062)　　　　USS Reasoner (DE-1063)　　　　USS Lockwood (DE-1064)

USS Stein (DE-1065)　　　　USS Marvin Shields (DE-1066)　　　　USS Francis Hammond (DE-1067)

DE

USS Vreeland (DE-1068)   USS Bagley (DE-1069)   USS Downes (DE-1070)

USS Badger (DE-1071)   USS Blakely (DE-1072)   USS Robert E. Peary (DE-1073)

USS Harold E. Holt (DE-1074)   USS Trippe (DE-1075)

DE

USS Fanning (DE-1076) USS Joseph Hewes (DE-1078) USS Bowen (DE-1079)

USS Paul (DE-1080)

USS Elmer Montgomery (DE-1082)

USS McCandless (DE-1084) USS Cook (DE-1083)

DE

USS Donald B. Beary (DE-1085)

USS Brewton (DE-1086)

USS Kirk (DE-1087)

USS Jesse L. Brown (DE-1089)

USS Ainsworth (DE-1090)

USS Barbey (DE-1088)

USS Miller (DE-1091)

DE

USS Thomas C. Hart (DE-1092)

USS Capodanno (DE-1093)

USS Pharris (DE-1094)

USS Valdez (DE-1096)

USS Moinester (DE-1097)

USS Truett (DE-1095)

USS Brooke (DEG-1)

DEG

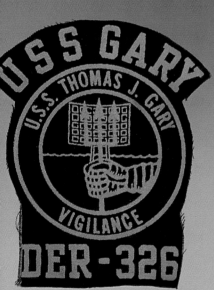

USS Ramsey (DEG-2)	USS Schofield (DEG-3)	USS Talbot (DEG-4)
USS Richard L. Page (DEG-5)	USS Julius A. Furer (DEG-6)	USS Falgout (DER-324)
USS Thomas J. Gary (DER-326)	USS Brister (DER-327)	USS Finch (DER-328)

DER

USS Kretchmer (DER-329)   USS Forster (DER-334)   USS Savage (DER-386)

USS Vance (DER-387)   USS Lansing (DER-388)   USS Calcaterra (DER-390)

USS Haverfield (DER-393)   USS Wilhoite (DER-397)

DER

USS Hissem (DER-400)

USS Mitscher (DL-2)

USS John S. McCain (DL-3)

USS Farragut (DLG-6)

USS Luce (DLG-7)

USS MacDonough (DLG-8)

USS Coontz (DLG-9)

USS King (DLG-10)

USS Mahan (DLG-11)

DLG

USS Dahlgren (DLG-12)	USS William V. Pratt (DLG-13)	USS Dewey (DLG-14)
USS Preble (DLG-15)	USS Harry E. Yarnell (DLG-17)	USS Richard K. Turner (DLG-20)
USS Gridley (DLG-21)	USS England (DLG-22)	USS Halsey (DLG-23)

DLG

USS Reeves (DLG-24)　　　　USS Belknap (DLG-26)　　　　USS Josephus Daniels (DLG-27)

USS Wainwright (DLG-28)　　　USS Jouett (DLG-29)　　　　USS Horne (DLG-30)

USS Sterett (DLG-31)　　　　USS William H. Standley (DLG-32)

DLG

| USS Fox (DLG-33) | USS Biddle (DLG-34) | USS Bainbridge (DLGN-25) |

USS Truxtun (DLGN-35)   USS California (DLGN-36)

USS South Carolina (DLGN-37)   USS Mississippi (EAG-128)   USS Compass Island (EAG-153)

EAG

USS Observation Island (EAG-154)

USF Constellation, Baltimore

USS Julius A. Furer (FF-6)

USS Bronstein (FF-1037)

USS McCloy (FF-1038)

USS Garcia (FF-1040)

USS Garcia (FF-1040), TASS

USS Garcia (FF-1040), Mediterranean Cruise, 1985

USS Bradley (FF-1041)

FF

USS Edward McDonnell (FF-1043)	USS Edward McDonnell (FF-1043)	USS Brumby (FF-1044)
USS Davidson (FF-1045)	USS Davidson (FF-1045)	USS Voge (FF-1047)
USS Sample (FF-1048)	USS Koelsch (FF-1049)	USS Albert David (FF-1050)

FF

USS O'Callahan (FF-1051)   USS O'Callahan (FF-1051)   USS Knox (FF-1052)

USS Knox (FF-1052)   USS Roark (FF-1053)   USS Roark (FF-1053)

USS Gray (FF-1054)   USS Hepburn (FF-1055)   USS Connole (FF-1056)

FF

USS Connole (FF-1056)   USS Rathburne (FF-1057)   USS Rathburne (FF-1057), Westpac, 1985

USS Meyerkord (FF-1058)   USS Meyerkord (FF-1058)   USS W.S. Sims (FF-1059)

USS Lang (FF-1060)   USS Patterson (FF-1061)   USS Patterson (FF-1061)

FF

USS Whipple (FF-1062)   USS Whipple (FF-1062)   USS Reasoner (FF-1063)

USS Reasoner (FF-1063)   USS Lockwood (FF-1064)   USS Lockwood (FF-1064)

USS Stein (FF-1065)   USS Stein (FF-1065)   USS Marvin Shields (FF-1066)

FF

USS Marvin Shields (FF-1066)   USS Francis Hammond (FF-1067)   USS Francis Hammond (FF-1067)

USS Vreeland (FF-1068)   USS Vreeland (FF-1068)   USS Vreeland (FF-1068), Mediterranean Cruise, 1991

USS Bagley (FF-1069)   USS Bagley (FF-1069)   USS Downes (FF-1070)

FF

USS Downes (FF-1070)   USS Downes (FF-1070), Westpac, 1990   USS Badger (FF-1071)

USS Badger (FF-1071)   USS Badger (FF-1071)   USS Blakely (FF-1072)

USS Blakely (FF-1072)   USS Robert E. Peary (FF-1073)   USS Robert E. Peary (FF-1073)

FF

USS Robert E. Peary (FF-1073),
Kangaroo EX, 1989

USS Harold E. Holt (FF-1074)

USS Harold E. Holt (FF-1074), Operation
Desert Shield, 1990

USS Harold E. Holt (FF-1074), Operation Desert Shield, 1990

USS Trippe (FF-1075)

USS Trippe (FF-1075)

USS Fanning (FF-1076)

USS Fanning (FF-1076)

USS Fanning (FF-1076)

FF

USS Ouellet (FF-1077)   USS Ouellet (FF-1077), Vodka Station, 1984   USS Joseph Hewes (FF-1078)

USS Joseph Hewes (FF-1078), Mediterranean/Indian Ocean, 1989   USS Bowen (FF-1079)   USS Bowen (FF-1079)

USS Bowen (FF-1079)   USS Bowen (FF-1079), Mediterranean Cruise, 1987   USS Paul (FF-1080)

FF

USS Paul (FF-1080), Decommissioning Crew, 1971-1992   USS Aylwin (FF-1081)   USS Aylwin (FF-1081)

USS Aylwin (FF-1081)   USS Aylwin (FF-1081)   USS Elmer Montgomery (FF-1082)

USS Elmer Montgomery (FF-1082)   USS Elmer Montgomery (FF-1082), Indian Ocean/Mediterranean/Atlantic, 1988

FF

USS Cook (FF-1083)   USS Cook (FF-1083)   USS McCandless (FF-1084)

USS McCandless (FF-1084)   USS Donald B. Beary (FF-1085)

USS Kirk (FF-1087)   USS Brewton (FF-1086)

FF

USS Barbey (FF-1088)

USS Jesse L. Brown (FF-1089)

USS Jesse L. Brown (FF-1089)

USS Jesse L. Brown (FF-1089), UNITAS XXX, 1989

USS Ainsworth (FF-1090)

USS Ainsworth (FF-1090)

USS Miller (FF-1091)

USS Miller (FF-1091)

FF

USS Thomas C. Hart (FF-1092)   USS Thomas C. Hart (FF-1092)   USS Thomas C. Hart (FF-1092)

USS Capodanno (FF-1093)   USS Capodanno (FF-1093), Mediterranean Cruise, 1993   USS Pharris (FF-1094)

USS Pharris (FF-1094)   USS Truett (FF-1095)

FF

USS Truett (FF-1095)	USS Valdez (FF-1096)	USS Valdez (FF-1096)
USS Moinester (FF-1097)	USS Glover (FF-1098)	USS Glover (FF-1098)
USS Brooke (FFG-1)	USS Ramsey (FFG-2)	USS Schofield (FFG-3)

FFG

USS Talbot (FFG-4)   USS Talbot (FFG-4)   USS Richard L. Page (FFG-5)

USS Richard L. Page (FFG-5)   USS Julius A. Furer (FFG-6)   USS Oliver Hazard Perry (FFG-7)

USS McInerney (FFG-8)   USS McInerney (FFG-8)   USS McInerney (FFG-8)

FFG

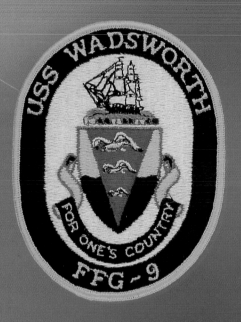

USS Wadsworth (FFG-9)   USS Wadsworth (FFG-9)   USS Wadsworth (FFG-9)

USS Wadsworth (FFG-9)   USS Wadsworth (FFG-9)   USS Duncan (FFG-10)

FFG

USS Duncan (FFG-10)   USS Duncan (FFG-10)   USS Clark (FFG-11)

USS George Philip (FFG-12)   USS Samuel Eliot Morison (FFG-13)   USS Sides (FFG-14)

USS Estocin (FFG-15)   USS Clifton Sprague (FFG-16)

FFG

USS Clifton Sprague (FFG-16)

USS John A. Moore (FFG-19)

USS John A. Moore (FFG-19), Persian Gulf

USS Antrim (FFG-20)

USS Antrim (FFG-20), Great Lakes Cruise, 1988

USS Flatley (FFG-21)

USS Flatley (FFG-21)

USS Flatley (FFG-21), SSDF

USS Fahrion (FFG-22)

FFG

USS Fahrion (FFG-22) USS Lewis B. Puller (FFG-23) USS Lewis B. Puller (FFG-23)

USS Jack Williams (FFG-24) USS Copeland (FFG-25) USS Gallery (FFG-26)

USS Gallery (FFG-26), Mideast Cruise, 1985-1986 USS Gallery (FFG-26), Persian Gulf, 1987

FFG

USS Gallery (FFG-26), Mediterranean Cruise, 1991   USS Gallery (FFG-26), Persian Gulf, 1993   USS Gallery (FFG-26), Persian Gulf, 1995

USS Mahlon S. Tisdale (FFG-27)   USS Mahlon S. Tisdale (FFG-27), Just Cruising   USS Boone (FFG-28)

USS Boone (FFG-28)   USS Boone (FFG-28), Mediterranean Cruise, 1992

FFG

USS Stephen W. Groves (FFG-29)   USS Stephen W. Groves (FFG-29), Red Sea/Mediterranean, 1992 USS Reid (FFG-30)   USS Reid (FFG-30)

USS Reid (FFG-30), Westpac, 1992-1993   USS Stark (FFG-31)

USS Stark (FFG-31), Persian Gulf, 1991-1992   USS Stark (FFG-31), UNITAS XXXIV, 1993   USS Stark (FFG-31), Persian Gulf, 1995

FFG

USS John L. Hall (FFG-32)   USS Jarrett (FFG-33)   USS Aubrey Fitch (FFG-34)

USS Aubrey Fitch (FFG-34)   USS Underwood (FFG-36)   USS Underwood (FFG-36)

USS Underwood (FFG-36), Persian Gulf, 1991   USS Crommelin (FFG-37)

FFG

USS Curts (FFG-38)   USS Curts (FFG-38)   USS Curts (FFG-38), Operation Desert Storm, 1990-1991

USS Curts (FFG-38)   USS Doyle (FFG-39)   USS Doyle (FFG-39)

USS Doyle (FFG-39), North Atlantic Cruise   USS Doyle (FFG-39), North Atlantic Cruise, 1993

FFG

USS Halyburton (FFG-40)   USS Halyburton (FFG-40), Persian Gulf, 1988 USS Halyburton (FFG-40)

USS Halyburton (FFG-40), Line Of Death, Libya, 1986 USS Halyburton (FFG-40), Operation Desert Storm, 1991

USS Halyburton (FFG-40), Mediterranean Cruise, 1992-1993 USS McClusky (FFG-41), Plank Owner USS McClusky (FFG-41)

FFG

USS McClusky (FFG-41)   USS McClusky (FFG-41), Westpac, 1986   USS McClusky (FFG-41), Middle East Force, 1987-1988

USS Klakring (FFG-42)   USS Klakring (FFG-42), Persian Gulf, 1987   USS Thach (FFG-43)

USS Thach (FFG-43)   USS De Wert (FFG-45)   USS De Wert (FFG-45), Persian Gulf, 1989

FFG

USS De Wert (FFG-45), Mediterranean Cruise, 1991   USS Rentz (FFG-46)   USS Nicholas (FFG-47)

USS Nicholas (FFG-47)   USS Nicholas (FFG-47), Persian Gulf, 1988   USS Nicholas (FFG-47), Second "E",
                                                                                    Battenburg Cup, 1988

USS Vandegrift (FFG-48)   USS Vandegrift (FFG-48)

FFG

USS Vandegrift (FFG-48), Westpac, 1990   USS Robert G. Bradley (FFG-49)   USS Taylor (FFG-50)

USS Gary (FFG-51)   USS Gary (FFG-51)   USS Carr (FFG-52)

USS Hawes (FFG-53)   USS Hawes (FFG-53)

FFG

USS Ford (FFG-54)

USS Ford (FFG-54)

USS Ford (FFG-54), Operation Desert Storm, 1990-1991

USS El Rod (FFG-55)

USS El Rod (FFG-55), Persian Gulf, 1989

USS El Rod (FFG-55), Arctic Circle/Equator, 1991-1992

USS Simpson (FFG-56)

USS Reuben James (FFG-57)

USS Reuben James (FFG-57)

FFG

USS Reuben James (FFG-57), Clean-EX, 1990   USS Samuel B. Roberts (FFG-58)   USS Samuel B. Roberts (FFG-58)

USS Samuel B. Roberts (FFG-58), Operation Desert Shield, 1990   USS Kauffman (FFG-59)   USS Kauffman (FFG-59)

USS Kauffman (FFG-59), Persian Gulf   USS Rodney M. Davis (FFG-60)   USS Rodney M. Davis (FFG-60)   USS Ingraham (FFG-61)
Fantasy Cruise, 1991

FFG

USS Ingraham (FFG-61)   USS Joseph Hewes (FFT-1078)   USS Joseph Hewes (FFT-1078)

USS Ainsworth (FFT-1090)   USS Truett (FFT-1095)   USS Constitution (IX-21)

USS Elk River (IX-501)

USS New Bedford (IX-308), cap patch   Helicopter Landing Trainer (IX-514)

IX

USS El Dorado (LCC-11)   USS Blue Ridge (LCC-19)   USS Blue Ridge (LCC-19)   USS Blue Ridge (LCC-19), Battle of Coral Sea, 50th Anniversary, 1942-1992

USS Mount Whitney (LCC-20)   USS Clarion River (LFR-409)   USS Algol (LKA-54)

USS Tulare (LKA-112)   USS Tulare (LKA-112), cap patch

LKA

USS Charleston (LKA-113) USS Charleston (LKA-113) USS Durham (LKA-114)

USS Durham (LKA-114) USS Mobile (LKA-115) USS Mobile (LKA-115)

USS Mobile (LKA-115), Operation Desert Shield, 1990-1991 USS St. Louis (LKA-116) USS St. Louis (LKA-116)

LKA

USS St. Louis (LKA-116), Westpac, 1975-1976

USS El Paso (LKA-117)

USS Paul Revere (LPA-248)

USS Francis Marion (LPA-249)

USS Raleigh (LPD-1)

USS Vancouver (LPD-2)

USS Vancouver (LPD-2)

USS La Salle (LPD-3)

USS Austin (LPD-4)

LPD

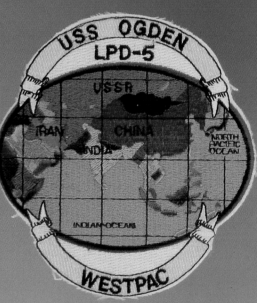

USS Austin (LPD-4)	USS Ogden (LPD-5)	USS Ogden (LPD-5)
USS Ogden (LPD-5), Westpac	USS Duluth (LPD-6)	USS Duluth (LPD-6)
USS Cleveland (LPD-7)	USS Cleveland (LPD-7)	USS Dubuque (LPD-8)

LPD

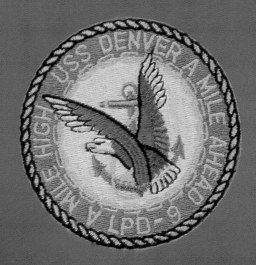

USS Dubuque (LPD-8)	USS Denver (LPD-9)	USS Denver (LPD-9)
USS Denver (LPD-9), Operation Desert Storm, 1990-1991	USS Juneau (LPD-10)	USS Juneau (LPD-10)
USS Coronado (LPD-11)	USS Shreveport (LPD-12)	USS Shreveport (LPD-12)

LPD

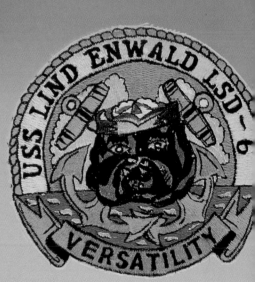

USS Nashville (LPD-13)	USS Trenton (LPD-14)	USS Trenton (LPD-14), Mediterranean Cruise, 1989-1990
USS Ponce (LPD-15)	USS Ashland (LSD-1)	USS Belle Grove (LSD-2)
USS Epping Forest (LSD-4)	USS Gunston Hall (LSD-5)	USS Lind Enwald (LSD-6)

LSD

USS Oak Hill (LSD-7)   USS Shadwell (LSD-15)   USS Cabildo (LSD-16)

USS Comstock (LSD-19)   USS Donner (LSD-20)   USS Fort Mandan (LSD-21)

USS Fort Marion (LSD-22)   USS San Marcos (LSD-25)

LSD

USS Whetstone (LSD-27)

USS Thomaston (LSD-28)

USS Thomaston (LSD-28)

USS Plymouth Rock (LSD-29)

USS Plymouth Rock (LSD-29)

USS Plymouth Rock (LSD-29)

USS Fort Snelling (LSD-30)

USS Point Defiance (LSD-31)

USS Spiegel Grove (LSD-32)

LSD

USS Alamo (LSD-33)	USS Hermitage (LSD-34)	USS Monticello (LSD-35)
USS Anchorage (LSD-36)	USS Anchorage (LSD-36)	USS Portland (LSD-37)
USS Portland (LSD-37)	USS Portland (LSD-37)	USS Pensacola (LSD-38)

LSD

USS Mount Vernon (LSD-39) USS Mount Vernon (LSD-39), Operation Desert Storm, 1990-1991 USS Fort Fisher (LSD-40)

USS Whidbey Island (LSD-41) USS Germantown (LSD-42) USS Germantown (LSD-42), Operation Desert Storm, 1990-1991

USS Fort McHenry (LSD-43) USS Gunston Hall (LSD-44) USS Comstock (LSD-45)

LSD

USS Tortuga (LSD-46) USS Rushmore (LSD-47) USS Ashland (LSD-48)

USS Harpers Ferry (LSD-49) USS Carter Hall (LSD-50) USS Duval County (LST-758)

USS Garrett County (LST-786) USS Hunterdon County (LST-838)

LST

USS Kemper County (LST-854)   USS Litchfield County (LST-901)   USS Luzerne County (LST-902)

USS Page County (LST-1076)   USS Park County (LST-1077)   USS San Joaquin County (LST-1122)

USS Snohomish County (LST-1126)   USS Stark County (LST-1134)   USS Stone County (LST-1141)

LST

USS Talbot County (LST-1153)   USS Tallahatchie County (LST-1154)   USS Terrebonne Parish (LST-1156)

USS Tioga County (LST-1158)   USS Tom Green County (LST-1159)

USS Vernon County (LST-1161)   USS Waldo County (LST-1163)   USS Waldo County (LST-1163)

LST

USS Washoe County (LST-1165)

USS Westchester County (LST-1167)

USS Washtenaw County (LST-1166)

USS Wexford County (LST-1168)

USS Whitfield County (LST-1169)

USS Windham County (LST-1170)

USS DeSoto County (LST-1171)

LST

USS Suffolk County (LST-1173)   USS Grant County (LST-1174)   USS York County (LST-1175)

USS York County (LST-1175)   USS York County (LST-1175)   USS Lorain County (LST-1176)

USS Newport (LST-1179)   USS Wood County (LST-1178)   USS Newport (LST-1179)

LST

USS Manitowoc (LST-1180)   USS Sumter (LST-1181)

USS Fresno (LST-1182)   USS Fresno (LST-1182)   USS Fresno (LST-1182)

USS Peoria (LST-1183)   USS Peoria (LST-1183)   USS Frederick (LST-1184)

LST

USS Frederick (LST-1184)

USS Schenectady (LST-1185)

USS Schenectady (LST-1185)

USS Schenectady (LST-1185)

USS Cayuga (LST-1186)

USS Cayuga (LST-1186)

USS Cayuga (LST-1186)

USS Tuscaloosa (LST-1187)

USS Saginaw (LST-1188)

LST

USS Saginaw (LST-1188), UNITAS Cruise XXVI, 1985   USS San Bernardino (LST-1189)   USS San Bernardino (LST-1189)

USS San Bernardino (LST-1189)   USS Boulder (LST-1190)   USS Racine (LST-1191)

USS Racine (LST-1191)   USS Racine (LST-1191)

LST

USS Spartanburg County (LST-1192)   USS Spartanburg County (LST-1192)   USS Fairfax County (LST-1193)

USS Fairfax County (LST-1193)   USS Lamoure County (LST-1194)   USS Lamoure County (LST-1194), UNITAS XXXV, 1994

USS Barbour County (LST-1195)   USS Barbour County (LST-1195), Southern Pacific, 1987   USS Harlan County (LST-1196)

LST

USS Barnstable County (LST-1197)   USS Bristol County (LST-1198)

USS Barnstable County (LST-1197), Operation Smokey Topaz, 1982

USS Bristol County (LST-1198)   USS Avenger (MCM-1)   USS Defender (MCM-2)

USS Sentry (MCM-3)   USS Champion (MCM-4)   USS Guardian (MCM-5)

MCM

USS Guardian (MCM-5), Operation Desert Storm, 1991

USS Devasator (MCM-6)

USS Patriot (MCM-7)

USS Scout (MCM-8)

USS Gladiator (MCM-11)

USS Ardent (MCM-12)

USS Dextrous (MCM-13)

USS Chief (MCM-14)

USS Catskill (MCS-1)

MCS

USS Ozark (MCS-2)

USS Epping Forest (MCS-7)

USS Osprey (MHC-51)

USS Frigate Bird (MSC-191)

USS Vireo (MSC-205)

USS Heron (MHC-52), Plankowner

USS Whippoorwill (MSC-207)

USS Linnet (MSCO-24)

MSCO

USS Conflict (MSO-426)   USS Constant (MSO-427)   USS Constant (MSO-427), Persian Gulf

USS Dash (MSO-428)   USS Detector (MSO-429)   USS Direct (MSO-430)

USS Direct (MSO-430)   USS Dominant (MSO-431), cap patch   USS Engage (MSO-433)

MSO

USS Enhance (MSO-437)   USS Enhance (MSO-437)   USS Excel (MSO-439)

USS Excel (MSO-439)   USS Exultant (MSO-441)   USS Fearless (MSO-442)

USS Fearless (MSO-442)   USS Fidelity (MSO-443)   USS Fortify (MSO-446)

MSO

USS Illusive (MSO-448)

USS Illusive (MSO-448)

USS Implicit (MSO-455)

USS Inflict (MSO-456)

USS Pluck (MSO-464)

USS Pluck (MSO-464)

USS Pluck (MSO-464)

USS Salute (MSO-470)

USS Conquest (MSO-488)

MSO

USS Gallant (MSO-489)   USS Gallant (MSO-489)   USS Pledge (MSO-492)   USS Adroit (MSO-509)

USS Affray (MSO-511)   USS Washtenaw County (MSS-2), Hai-Phong Harbor Check Sweep   USS Cambria (PA-36)

USS Cyclone (PC-1)   USS Tempest (PC-2)   USS Hurricane (PC-3)   USS Monsoon (PC-4)

PC

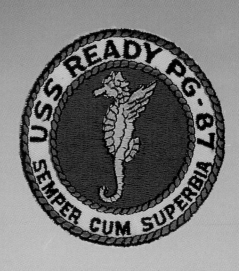

USS Sirocco (PC-6)	USS Squall (PC-7)	USS Zephyr (PC-8)
USS Havre (PCE-877)	USS High Point (PCH-1)	USS Hollidaysburg (PCS-1385)
USS Gallup (PG-85)	USS Antelope (PG-86)	USS Ready (PG-87)

PG

USS Crockett (PG-88) USS Marathon (PG-89) USS Canon (PG-90)

USS Tacoma (PG-92) USS Welch (PG-93)

USS Surprise (PG-97), Mediterranean Cruise, 1970-1971 USS Grand Rapids (PG-98) USS Beacon (PG-99)

PG

USS Green Bay (PG-101)   USS Flagstaff (PGH-1)   USS Crockett (PGM-88)

USS Pegasus (PHM-1)   USS Hercules (PHM-2)   USS Taurus (PHM-3)

USS Aquila (PHM-4)   USS Aries (PHM-5)   USS Gemini (PHM-6)

PHM

USS Ferret (TWR-6)   USS George Eastman (YAG-39)   USS Granville S. Hall (YAG-40)

USS Monob (YAG-61)   USS Interceptor (YAGR-8)

USS Investigator (YAGR-Division 21)   USS Investigator (YAGR-Division 21)

YAGR

USS Interpreter (YAGR-11)   USS Delta Queen (YFR-890)   USS —— (YFRT-451)

USS —— (YFRT-520), NUWES, Keyport

USS Apopka (YTB-778)   USS Defiance (—)   USS Sulaco (—)

YTB

INDEX

INDEX

INDEX

GLOSSARY

Around the Horn	Cape Horn, South America
ASW	Anti-Submarine Warfare
B.I.O.T.	British Indian Ocean Territory
Blue Nose	North Atlantic
CTF	Commander Task Force
"E"	Battle Readiness Award
HornEx	Cape Horn Exercise
I.O.	Indian Ocean
JTG	Joint Task Group
Med	Mediterranean Sea
MEF	Middle East Force
MidPac	Mid Pacific
MIF	Maritime Interdiction Force
NorLant	Northern Atlantic
NorPac	Northern Pacific
Pacex	Pacific Exercise
Plankowner	An individual that was on Board at commissioning
RimPac	Pacific Rim
"S"	Safety Award
SNFL	Standard Naval Force Atlantic
Sunset Cruise	Scheduled for Decommissioning on return
TASS	Towed Array Sonar System (ASW)
The Ditch	Suez Canal
Unitas	Annual joint exercise with South America
WestPac	Western Pacific